D1348364

SEREN JAMES

the little book of
LEADERSHIP

Hero, 51 Gower Street, London, WC1E 6HJ
hero@hero-press.com | www.hero-press.com

Contents © Seren James 2020
The right of the above author to be identified as the author of this work has
been asserted in accordance with the Copyright, Designs and Patents Act 1988.
British Library Cataloguing in Publication Data available.

Print ISBN 978-1-78955-1-235
Ebook ISBN 978-1-78955-1-242
Set in Times and Futura.

Preface

A leader is someone appointed to guide and influence others to achieve an objective or goal. Whether in the workplace, education, sport or social activity, having a clear vision and the will to succeed is something all good leaders strive for.

This handy pocket-size book contains inspirational quotes to motivate and help you lead the way whatever your goal or objective may be. A refreshingly simple and easy-to-read book, as well as being wonderfully thought-provoking.

Leadership

A great leader wants
everyone to succeed
not just for themselves

The price of greatness is responsibility

WINSTON CHURCHILL

Motivate and inspire
through your actions

I cannot teach anybody
anything, I can only
make them think

SOCRATES

Opportunities multiply as they are seized

SUN TZU

Passion for your role will motivate others to follow your lead

It is beyond a doubt
that all our knowledge
begins with experience

IMMANUEL KANT

The superior man is
modest in his speech
but excels in his actions

CONFUCIUS

Tell me and I forget,
teach me and I
remember, involve me
and I learn

BENJAMIN FRANKLIN

If there is any one secret
of success, it lies in the
ability to get the other
person's point of view
and see things from that
person's angle as well
as from your own

HENRY FORD

Inspire others to take the lead and you will get a motivated workforce

When you are content
to be simply yourself
and don't compare or
compete, everybody
will respect you

LAOZI

Have clear
communication and
ensure everyone
understands

Choose always the way that seems the best, however rough it may be; custom will soon render it easy and agreeable

PYTHAGORAS

A positive attitude goes
a long way

For success, attitude is
equally as important
as ability

WALTER SCOTT

Innovate and evolve
your thoughts

For a man to conquer
himself is the first and
noblest of all victories

PLATO

Brush up on your skills
and resources

The great aim of
education is not
knowledge but action

HERBERT SPENCER

Have a vision for the future and you will always be relevant

The well-bred contradict
other people. The wise
contradict themselves

OSCAR WILDE

Integrity is the most
valuable and respected
quality of leadership

He who fears being
conquered is sure
of defeat

NAPOLEON BONAPARTE

Keep your team focused,
encourage them with
motivational words
or rewards

He that cannot obey, cannot command

BENJAMIN FRANKLIN

Have a vision,
have a plan and
make it happen

I never expect to see a
perfect work from an
imperfect man

ALEXANDER HAMILTON

Leaders are made,
not born

The most useless are
those who never
change through
the years

J.M. BARRIE

Motivate and inspire
through your actions

Compromise makes a
good umbrella but a
poor roof

JAMES RUSSELL LOWELL

Listen to ideas and be
open to change

If you wish to win a man
over to your ideas, first
make him your friend

ABRAHAM LINCOLN

Learn how to listen.
Really listen. Only then
will you be able to lead

There are some defeats more triumphant than victories

MICHEL DE MONTAIGNE

Always be honest
with your thoughts
and opinions

Experience is the
teacher of all things

JULIUS CAESAR

A leader always
sees the potential,
not the obstacle

Energy and persistence
conquer all things

BENJAMIN FRANKLIN

Offer a plan or
solution that everyone
understands

Coming together is a
beginning. Keeping
together is progress.
Working together
is success

HENRY FORD

The value of an idea
lies in the using of it

THOMAS EDISON

To lead is to unlock
potential in others
and encourage them
to be the best

The will to win, the desire
to succeed, the urge to
reach your full potential...
these are the keys that
will unlock the door to
personal excellence

CONFUCIUS

If you believe in your
team, your team will
believe in you

Make the best use of what's in your power and take the rest as it happens

EPICTETUS

Leaders get results,
not excuses

He who is not a good
servant will not be a
good master

PLATO

If you are committed
to the cause, then your
team will be too

Mastering others is
strength. Mastering
yourself is true power

LAOZI

A sign of a good
leader is not how
many followers you
have but how many
leaders you create

MAHATMA GANDHI

Leadership is not a
position or a title, it is
action and example

ANON

Let your team rise
to the occasion

Assess your team, iron
out negativity, change
or alter skill sets if
necessary, to reach
your goal

You can do what I
cannot do. I can do
what you cannot do.
Together we can do
great things

MOTHER TERESA

Pleasure in the job puts
perfection in the work

ARISTOTLE

Have convictions. Be friendly. Stick to your beliefs as they stick to theirs. Work as hard as they do

ELEANOR ROOSEVELT

You don't develop
courage by being happy
in your relationships
everyday. You develop it
by surviving difficult times
and challenging adversity

EPICURUS

Leaders see opportunity
in situations rather
than the difficulty of
the situation

Leaders create change
and encourage
innovation

Always recognize that human individuals are ends, and do not use them as means to your end

IMMANUEL KANT

If the performance is
poor, change the way
it is being done

Find the right role and
you'll get the right results

Give them confidence
that they can do the job
and the job will
be done

No man will make a
great leader who wants
to do it all himself, or to
get all the credit
for doing it

ANDREW CARNEGIE

Be the example to
set the example

Adopt different
approaches to achieve
each step towards
your goal

To accomplish great things,
we must not only act,
but also dream,
not only plan,
but also believe

ANATOLE FRANCE

Break down the task –
a little goes a long way

A positive approach
brings creativity

Only when there are
things a man will not do
is he capable of doing
great things

MENCIUS

Encourage everyone
to be involved; only by
being involved will they
want to succeed

Have all the resources and tools to hand; this will avoid any excuses and delays

To understand the true
quality of people,
you must look into
their minds, and
examine their pursuits
and aversions

MARCUS AURELIUS

Have realistic timelines
and targets that
are achievable

Forget the risk and take
the fall; if it's what you
want then it's worth it all

ANON

Avoid misunderstanding

Haste in every business brings failures

HERODOTUS

Note that some of the team will not want full responsibility; do not think less of them: they will add value in another way. Find it.

Create and share
your vision

Get to know your team and their skills

Strategy without tactics
is the slowest route to
victory. Tactics without
strategy is the noise
before defeat

SUN TZU

Be focused on the task
and set yourself as an
example

A teacher affects
eternity; he can
never tell where
his influence stops

HENRY ADAMS

Have accountability
and teach responsibility

The best is he who calls
men to the best. And
those who heed the call
are also blessed. But
worthless who call not,
heed not, but rest

HESIOD

Be the inspiration and
direct them to success

You might need to
change your approach
or modify the objective
to get to the end result

Create a good
working culture

Know how to listen and you will profit even from those who talk badly

PLUTARCH

Never ignore
your gut feeling

Have enthusiasm and convictions in your vision and plans

Never tell people how to do things. Tell them what to do, and they will surprise you with their ingenuity

GEORGE S. PATTON

Listen to negative or
reluctant opinions,
sound them out

He who wishes to be
obeyed must know how
to command

NICCOLÒ MACHIAVELLI

Don't get angry or
frustrated: talk it out
and find a solution

Do something different
– clear the air and find
a new perspective

Anyone can be a
leader – to be a good
leader is something
else entirely

Quality is not an act,
it's a habit

ARISTOTLE

You can't plan for every
negative influence

Always refresh your skills and those of your workforce – learning never stops

Vary your leadership
style to suit each
situation

There is no such thing as
a big challenge

Nearly all men can stand adversity, but if you want to test a man's character, give him power

ABRAHAM LINCOLN

Whatever their thinking
– or lack of thinking –
be upfront

The one thing that matters is the effort

ANTOINE DE SAINT-EXUPÉRY

Positive thinking is
all powerful and will
overcome any obstacle

To do the same thing
over and over again
is not only boredom:
it is to be controlled by
rather than to control
what you do

HERACLITUS

Inject enthusiasm to
empower action

Always share credit,
emphasize team over self
and define success
collectively rather
than individually

You can't depend on
your eyes when your
imagination is out
of focus

MARK TWAIN

Keep calm, win trust
and be honest

Being a good leader takes time and dedication

Do not follow where
the path may lead. Go
instead where there is no
path and leave a trail

RALPH WALDO EMERSON

Excessive ego or concerns about status will hinder leadership qualities

Silence is better than unmeaning words

PYTHAGORAS

Take time to reflect if you want to go in the right direction

Men often become what
they believe themselves
to be. If I believe I cannot
do something, it makes me
incapable of doing it. But
when I believe I can, then
I acquire the ability to do
it even if I didn't have it in
the beginning

MAHATMA GANDHI

If your actions inspire
others to dream more,
learn more, do more
and become more,
you are a leader

JOHN QUINCY ADAMS

The mind is not a vessel
to be filled but a fire to
be kindled

PLUTARCH